Stunning
Castles
of Scotland

Photography by Graeme Wallace

ACKNOWLEDGEMENTS

Photography by **Graeme Wallace**
Designed by **Melvin Creative**
Reprographics by **GWP Graphics**
Printed by **Printer Trento, Italy**

Published by **GW Publishing**,
PO Box 6091, Thatcham, Berks, RG19 8XZ.
Tel + 44 (0)1635 268080
www.gwpublishing.com

First Published 2007

© *Copyright GW Publishing*

Photographs © Copyright Graeme Wallace.

All rights reserved. No part of this publication may be reproduced, stored in a retrieval system or transmitted in any form by any means electronic, mechanical, photocopy or otherwise without the prior permission in writing of the copyright owners.

ISBN 978 0 9551564 8 9

To order other publications visit www.gwpublishing.com

Front Cover, Dunvegan Castle
Page 1, Caerlaverock Castle
Page 4, Entrance to Culzean Castle

Back Cover, Castle Tioram
Page 2, Castle Campbell
Page 6, Portcullis Gate of Edinburgh Castle

In selecting the castles to be included in the book, the priority has been given to buildings that have been erected in stunning and beautiful locations as opposed to those with only great defensive attributes or stately value. I have endeavoured to capture the castles at their most striking, showing them in their surroundings at the most dramatic time of day.

For more detailed coverage of a wider selection of Scottish castles please see our book -
Scottish Castles & Fortifications ISBN 978 0 9546701 1 5

CONTENTS

Enjoying a rugged and mountainous coastline of more than 6,000 miles, Scotland can lay claim to having some of the most breathtaking castle locations in the world with many of these overlook its coastal waters.

Scotland has had a turbulent and volatile history as a result of the patriarchal clan system, with family feuds and rivalries, together with long struggles with other countries: most notably its southern neighbour England. It was, however, the inter clan and family fighting plus persistent invaders and raiders from overseas rather than England that largely influenced the erection of the majority of the great castles in this book.

Due to Scotland's rugged and isolated terrain, it was virtually impossible to control the country under one king or family, so for centuries the larger clans were often left to manage their own affairs. There was great loyalty and allegiance between the clan and their chief. The chief offered to provide, lead and protect his people, and the clan members followed him unflinchingly. The chief and the clan members were usually related by birth and had an unbreakable bond, further strengthening the position of the chief. Some of these chiefs ruled like kings and built castles to manage and control their lands. Inevitably conflict arose between different clans and families.

The obvious reason for building a castle was to protect the clan chief, lord or nobleman and their people. A castle was also used as a base from where to implement and enforce law, to house soldiers and imprison enemies, and also as a means of asserting and demonstrating power, wealth and authority. Some of Scotland's greatest castles were started in the eleventh and twelfth centuries, such as the magnificent Caerlaverock Castle, while many strongholds were occupied and developed over many centuries. The need for the defensive attributes of castles and tower houses diminished following the joining of the kingdoms Scotland and England under the Scottish king James VI in 1603 and then the Union of Parliaments in 1707. Many clan chiefs, lairds and landowners abandoned their cramped and basic castles for elegant new mansions and country houses, while others extended and remodelled their old fortresses into more comfortable residences.

From the beginning of time, man has taken advantage of natural defensive sites, and Scotland certainly offered unlimited opportunities. From mounds and hill tops to volcanic plugs and cliff-top promontories, there were ample vantage points on which to build. These sites needed secure water supplies and were strategically located to dominate the sea ways or land.

Although there may be little evidence of early building or defences, many of the castles in this book were built on sites on which an earlier, even prehistoric, stronghold stood. Indeed there is plenty of evidence to show that there has been a fortification on the site of the present Edinburgh Castle since the Iron Age. As siege methods improved, so did the design of castles, resulting in more inaccessible and defensible sites being chosen and engineered. Thicker walls, higher towers and defensive outer walls all led to the construction of stronger and more magnificent castles, including those along Scotland's western coastline and on the islands.

During this time, the sea was often the primary means of transport, so watching over sea ways was vitally important. Building a castle on the waters' edge enabled the occupants to observe the sea ways and communicate with neighbouring strongholds, as well as taking advantage of the natural defences and supply routes offered by the sea. Better still was to build on a peninsula or even on a small island. Consequently, the clan chiefs and Lowland lords often had castles impregnable to all but the most-determined and well-equipped foes. And few castles in the world can equal such dramatic and stunning locations.

The epitome of a dramatic castle surrounded by stunning scenery is Eilean Donan Castle. Standing on a small island overlooking three lochs, Eilean Donan was built by Alexander II, King of Scots in 1230 to defend against the Danes. It was long held by the Mackenzies of Kintail. However, even more remote, and possibly founded as early as the eleventh century, is Kisimul Castle in the Outer Hebrides. The base for Clan MacNeil, the castle was built on a rocky island in a bay off the southern coast of Barra. Castle Stalker can also lay claim to having the most stunning setting, standing as it does on a small island in the Lynn of Lorn with the brooding hills of Morvern as a backdrop.

Then there are the majestic, strategically important and powerful royal strongholds of Edinburgh and Stirling. Vying for prominence, each was built on a volcanic rock, and they dominated the surrounding landscape and the people who dwelt there. Both were the focus of repeated attacks, as both the Scots and English saw these castles as symbols of ultimate power over Scotland. Many smaller castles and towers were not built to withstand a full-scale attack, but were used to protect lords and landowners against local skirmishes and raids, as well as being lookout posts. On both sides of the border between England and Scotland were many tower houses and castles, with Smailholm Tower one of those ideally situated for maximum defence and vista.

Many of these defences were put to the test during the Wars of Independence and the long struggles with England. Most castles in Scotland are now ruined but some such as Edinburgh, Stirling, Eilean Donan and Kisimul survived the ravages of war or have been tastefully restored to their former glory, doing a great service to Scottish tourism.

Despite the troubles following the disastrous Jacobite Rising of 1745-46 which ended in the slaughter of Culloden, many clan chiefs were able to, and have continued to, hold on to their lands. Dunvegan Castle, on the western shore of the Isle of Skye, has been the seat of the MacLeods for more than 700 years, while Duart Castle on the Isle of Mull has been the seat of the chiefs of the Clan MacLean since the thirteenth century, although it had to be rebuilt from ruin in the twentieth century.

One of the most powerful families of Scotland in the thirteenth century was the Comyns. They were responsible for building many great castles that were vital to maintaining their power in the Highlands, such as Blair, Balvenie and Ruthven, the latter now demolished and replaced by a government barracks. The grand structure of Blair Castle in Perthshire was built around the original Comyn's Tower of 1269, but the property passed to the Stewart and then the Murray Earls and Dukes of Atholl.

As calmer times ensued following the Union of Scotland and England and the failure of the Jacobite Risings, the need for defences diminished, although the desire to demonstrate status and power never waned. Crathes Castle illustrates this change in attitude with magnificent aesthetic features, including decoratively carved and painted ceilings. The desire to live in more comfortable surroundings and to be in a more prosperous locations led Sir Duncan Campbell to totally demolish his original clan seat and build the grand Inveraray Castle many miles to the south with better access to the sea.

ISLAND RETREATS

Kisimul Castle *(below)*

Possibly dating from as early as the eleventh century, Kisimul Castle was
built by Clan MacNeil on a rock in the centre of a bay on the south coast of
Barra. The curtain wall encloses the entire island, making the castle virtually
impregnable, while the clan's birlinns (galleys) could be moored in the
shelter of the walls..

Castle Stalker *(opposite)*

Stark and remote, Castle Stalker is a simple tower built in a very dramatic
location on the Rock of the Cormorants at the mouth of Loch Laich. Built
on an islet for shelter and protection, access can only be made by boat.

Castle Stalker *(pages 10 / 15)*

Castle Stalker *(pages 11-14)*

Castle Tioram

Dating from 1230, Eilean Donan Castle stands on a rocky island at the junction of three lochs feeding into the north-west Highlands. First built by Alexander II, King of Scots, to defend Scotland against the Danes, it was also used by the Jacobites during their first campaign in 1719, when it was blown up. The castle was rebuilt from ruin in the early twentieth century, making it one of the most photogenic castles in Scotland and the setting for many blockbuster movies, including James Bond.

Eilean Donan Castle (opposite)

Eilean Donan Castle (pages 22-23)

prison of Mary, Queen of Scots. Mary was imprisoned in the keep in 1567 but was rescued the following year by a young squire who immobilised all the boats except his own vessel and used the well-proven technique of plying the garrison with alcohol.

Kilchurn Castle

Loch an Eilean Castle

At the foot of the Cairngorms, the thirteenth-century stronghold of the
Wolf of Badenoch sits in a loch on a tiny island no bigger than the castle
itself. The loch is surrounded by the ancient Caledonian forest of the

COASTAL FORTRESSES

St Andrews Castle (*above*)

Built on a coastal promontory, St Andrews Castle is protected on one side by the sea while a deep moat protected it on the landward side. Well defended, it was the scene of one of the longest, most bloody and bitter sieges in Scotland's history. The siege was eventually brought to an end after a year of fighting by the arrival of a fleet of French ships.

Brodick Castle (*opposite*)

In a position overlooking Brodick Bay on the Island of Arran, Brodick Castle was built on the site of a former Viking fortification. Starting out as a basic tower, it, like so many castles across Scotland, was considerably extended in the seventeenth century to make it a more comfortable residence, and was then remodelled in later centuries into a magnificent castle and mansion.

Blackness Castle *(below)*

The ship that never sailed.

Blackness is an ominous fortress with walls up to seventeen-foot thick and is further protected on three sides by the cold waters of the Firth of Forth. It was one of the strongest castles in central Scotland and is still very much intact. When built in 1440, the Lord Admiral of Scotland promised James II that he would build a ship that could not sink; when viewed from the east the castle does indeed resemble a ship.

Dunnottar Castle *(opposite)*

The rock of Dunnottar has been used a fortress from the earliest times, and a siege is recorded as having taken place here in 681 AD. Although now mostly ruinous, Dunnottar Castle still stands securely on an inaccessible rocky outcrop protruding into the North Sea on Scotland's north-east coast. With shear cliffs on all sides, it is virtually cut off from the mainland, making it a formidable fortress. Understandably, Dunnottar was the last castle in Scotland to fall to Cromwell's forces during the Civil War.

Dunnottar Castle *(pages 34 / 39)*

Dunnottar Castle *(pages 35-38)*

Urquhart Castle *(above)*

Holding a commanding position on Strone Point, a rocky promontory half
way along Loch Ness, Urquhart Castle enjoys views almost the entire
length of the loch. Built on the site of an earlier stronghold, the present
castle dates back to 1230. The castle sits in a strategic position at the
meeting of two important routes through the Highlands. It played a
prominent part in the Wars of Independence, and then again in 1390
against an incursion by the MacDonald Lords of the Isles.

Urquhart Castle *(opposite)*

Urquhart Castle *(pages 42-43)*

Inveraray Castle (*previous page*)

Overlooking Loch Fyne, Inveraray Castle is a splendid Gothic structure. Confident and defiant, with conical topped circular drum towers on each corner, the castle stands proud, portraying an air of regal strength and reflects the power held by Clan Campbell at the time it was built in the eighteenth century. The seat of the Duke of Argyll, head of Clan Campbell, the clan base was moved from Innis Chonnel in Loch Fyne to near the present location in the early fifteenth century.

Culzean Castle (*above*)

Sitting atop a 100-foot cliff face, which is peppered with sea-carved caves and caverns, Culzean looks out across the busy Firth of Clyde to Arran and the Mull of Kintyre. Its defences are now purely decorative although its vantage position ensures a dramatic setting and it incorporates much of the fabric of an ancient castle of the Kennedys.

Culzean Castle (*opposite*)

Mingary Castle (*page 48-49*)

Mingary Castle, on the Ardnamurchan peninsula, is the most westerly stronghold on the mainland of Great Britain. Although it now appears remote, the lands of Ardnamurchan were once populous and rich. Tracing the rough hexagonal shape of the rocky outcrop upon which it stands, the castle's main entrance faces the sea.

Mingary Castle

was built to withstand the longest siege. The castle has been the seat of the
chiefs of Clan MacLeod since the 1270s.

Dunvegan Castle *(opposite)*

Dunrobin Castle (*opposite*)

The largest castle in the northern Highlands, Dunrobin watches over the Dornoch Firth from its elevated rocky spur on Scotland's north-eastern coastline. The current 'fairy tale castle' appearance masks the original defensive nature of the building and its long history, but its stunning architecture and beautiful gardens make it unique in Scotland.

Tantallon Castle (*previous page*)

Flanked by twin towers and with a impressive gatehouse, Tantallon Castle has a massive fifty-foot high and thirteen-foot thick curtain wall, which was further defended by a deep ditch, cut into sold rock, making the castle virtually impregnable from land and sea. This was one of the strongest castles in southern Scotland, although it was finally captured by Cromwell's forces in 1651 after a twelve-day siege. The castle had access to the sea via a precarious sea gate and has one of the deepest wells in Scotland.

Duart Castle (*below*)

Enjoying one of the finest defensive positions in Europe, the menacing bulk of Duart Castle is the ancestral seat of Clan MacLean. With walls over ten-foot thick, it was built upon a rocky outcrop on the peninsula overlooking Duart Bay. Dominating the Sound of Mull, the major sea way between Ireland and the western Scottish mainland, control of Duart Castle meant power and influence in western Scotland.

Edinburgh Castle (below)

Built on the summit of a volcanic plug, 443 foot (135m) above sea level, Edinburgh Castle dominates the landscape with views in all directions. The castle was key to controlling Scotland, and it changed hands many times between the English and the Scots. Only taken once by a direct assault, more devious methods were used on several occasion to seize the castle. In 1313 Thomas Randoph, Robert the Bruce's nephew and captain, scaled the rock and walls with just 30 men to surprise the English garrison and take the castle.

Edinburgh Castle (opposite)

Tiny St Margaret's Chapel was the only building spared when the rest of the castle was rendered ineffective for military use by Bruce in 1313, thus making the chapel the oldest part of the present castle.

Edinburgh Castle (pages 58/63)

The Half Moon Battery was added after the Lang Siege of 1567-73 to defend the castle against the modern age of the cannon.

Edinburgh Castle (pages 59-62)

Edinburgh Castle from Arthur's Seat *(above)*

Edinburgh Castle *(opposite)*

The Edinburgh Military Tattoo, started in 1950 and running annually for
three weeks in August, takes place on the Esplanade in front of the castle.

Doune Castle *(pages 66-67)*

Built on a strong site and with a commanding and prominent gatehouse
tower, Doune was a formidable castle and is considered to be the perfect
fourteenth-century fortress. The castle is in a strategic, elevated position
above the River Teith, and guarded major routes from east to west and from
south to north.

Stirling Castle *(below)*

Known as the 'Key to Scotland' because of its strategic location, Stirling Castle was built on an extinct volcanic plug overlooking the main route between northern and southern Scotland. The shear vertical rock on the south face gives the castle a lofty and commanding aspect. The castle has suffered sixteen major sieges and was at one time, during the wars for Scottish independence, the last major stronghold still in the control of the Scots. It was visited by many of the monarchs of Scotland. James II and James III were both born here, and Mary, Queen of Scots, was crowned in the castle's chapel in 1543.

Stirling Castle *(opposite)*

The gatehouse to the castle is flanked by two mighty round towers, which were added in 1510 as an additional line of defence.

Stirling Castle *(pages 70-71)*

Stirling Castle *(above)*

The Great Hall of 1500 was
painted in a bright yellow wash to
project the dynastic identity of the

Scottish forces used the castle against
Cromwell in 1651, after which it
was attacked and then seized.

Crichton Castle

Crichton Castle *(previous page)*

Standing above a bend in the Tyne Water, Crichton Castle was first built around 1375. Mary, Queen of Scots, attended a wedding here in 1562 and was later married to its owner, James Hepburn, the fourth Earl of Bothwell. The castle later passed to Francis Stewart, the next Earl, who extensively remodelled the castle with the addition of a unique diamond-faceted façade.

Balvenie Castle *(below)*

Built on a 'brae' by the Comyns, one of the most powerful families in thirteenth-century Scotland, Balvenie Castle sits above the River Fiddich in Speyside. Although now in a quiet and out-of-the-way spot, it was one of a string of castles which helped the Black Comyns control the rich lands of Strathspey and Aberdeenshire.

Castle Campbell *(opposite)*

Castle Gloom

Sitting high above a chasm in the Ochil Hills, Castle Campbell has a daunting aspect, and controls the old drove road between Fife and the North. Passing by marriage in 1481 to Colin Campbell, first Earl of Argyll, the castle was a safe but convenient base from where to visit and conduct business with the Stewart courts at Stirling, Edinburgh and in the Lowlands.

Caerlaverock Castle *(previous pages)*

Possibly the greatest remaining example of a medieval castle in Scotland, Caerlaverock has suffered many attacks since being first built in 1270. Built to a triangular plan in marshy ground on the edge of the Solway Firth and Nith Estuary, the castle still has a wet moat. There were round towers at two corners with a double-tower gatehouse at the third, which was further strengthened and remodelled in the fifteenth century.

Hermitage Castle *(above)*

Brooding Hermitage Castle defended the Scottish border and was known as 'the guard house of the bloodiest valley in Britain'. The building of the first castle in 1242 almost sparked an English invasion, when Henry II of England objected to the massive fortress being constructed so close to the border. With few windows and those it does have tiny, the shear vertical walls and connecting corner towers give a harsh, stark and impregnable appearance, enough to give any neighbour cause for concern.

Claypotts Castle *(opposite)*

Built in 1588 by John Strachan, Claypotts was designed to show off the family's new found wealth and success. Although it was never apparently attacked, the circular towers and shot-holes and gunloops provided a degree of security against raids by jealous neighbours and invading armies.

Corgarff Castle *(above)*

Stark and isolated, Corgarff Castle stands on a remote windswept hilltop on the edge of the Cairngorm Mountains. Watching over an important drove road, the castle was a strategic base in numerous disputes, but also found itself subject to attack from Highland raiders and rebels on a number of occasions

Castle Fraser *(opposite)*

Comfortably at ease with its surroundings, Castle Fraser is one of the great castles of Mar and is a good example of a castellated Renaissance house. It is one of the finest baronial homes in northern Europe, and dates from the fifteenth century, although it took more than sixty years to complete the remodelling of the building as it appears today.

Glamis Castle *(pages 84-85)*

Glamis stands on a site that was formerly used as a hunting lodge by the kings of Scotland. A place favoured by James V, he moved his court here for part of each year after he had deprived the family of the estate and executed Lady Glamis Glamis returned to the Lyon family, and in 1606 they were made Earls of Kinghorne and then later also Earls of Strathmore. The family retain ownership today. Although the main tower dates from the fifteenth century, the conical-topped turrets and "defensive" battlements were added in the seventeenth century.

Scone Palace *(pages 86-87)*

A splendid gothic revival mansion, built in 1802, Scone incorporates part of an older, fortified dwelling dating from the 1580s and is built in the site of a medieval abbey. Records show that the site had military significance in Roman times, being on the outer edge of the then known world. The presence of the Stone of Destiny, held here from the 930s until the end of the thirteenth century, ensured that Scone played a significant part in Scottish history as the crowning place of the Scottish monarchs.

Brodie Castle *(opposite)*

The castle dates from as early as the twelfth century, but was torched in 1645, when the inhabitants survived the burning of the building by sheltering in the vaulted basement. The castle was long held by the Brodies, even after ambitious extensions and renovations which almost bankrupted the family, but is now in the care of The National Trust for Scotland.

Craigmillar Castle *(pages 92-93)*

Conveniently located near to Edinburgh, Craigmillar Castle is in a commanding position and stands on a hill with excellent views to the south. Acting as a first line of defence for the capital, Craigmillar is in sight of Edinburgh Castle and the two could communicate using beacon braziers and flashing mirrors.

Fyvie Castle *(below)*

Fyvie Castle sits above the river Ythan and dates back to medieval times. Fyvie was at one time a strong fortress but it has been remodelled and extended over 500 years into a magnificent domestic residence, with each of its five towers being added by the different families who owned it. The central twin drum towers were added in the seventeenth century.

Craigmillar Castle

Crathes Castle (below)

Designed as both a fortified
residence and a symbol of baronial
confidence, Crathes Castle typifies
the 'new' attitude towards castle
building: a grand domestic home
with comfort and ornament as well
as a defensive base secure from
neighbours. Built in 1553 by the
Burnetts, the castle replaced their
earlier stronghold which stood on
an island in the middle of the Loch
of Leys.

Crathes Castle (opposite)

Drummond Castle *(below)*

Standing proud overlooking splendid gardens, Drummond Castle was built at the close of the fifteenth century on lands near Crieff in Perthshire. The family came to prominence after Sir Malcolm Drummond distinguished himself in 1314 at the Battle of Bannockburn when in the army of Robert the Bruce that crushed the English.

Drum Castle *(opposite)*

No one can deny the strength of the original tower of Drum Castle, although there are no natural defences. The walls of the old part are twelve-foot thick and the entrance was positioned on the first floor and was accessed by an external retractable wooden ramp.

Blair Castle *(pages 98/103)*

Strategically built to guard the road north through the Drumochter Pass into the rugged Highlands, Blair Castle enjoys a mountainous backdrop and is surrounded by wooded hills. Originally a simple tower, the castle has been extensively enlarged since first being built in 1269, and has remained in the ownership of the Earls, Marquises and Dukes of Atholl since the thirteenth century.

Blair Castle *(pages 99-102)*

With turrets on each corner of the tower, it was heavily fortified although the seventeenth-century remodelling disguising its defences. The entrance is reached across a drawbridge spanning the deep ditch.

Floors Castle *(previous pages)*

The largest inhabited mansion in Scotland, Floors Castle sits above the north bank of the River Tweed. From a rather bland country house, the celebrated architect William Playfair transformed the building into the magnificent palace of today. The property has been long owned by the Kerr family, now the Dukes of Roxburghe.

Neidpath Castle *(above)*

Overlooking a steep bank on a bend of the River Tweed, Neidpath Castle is one of the many castles and tower house which defended the border area with England. Neidpath holds the honour of holding out longer against the army of Cromwell than any other fortress in southern Scotland during the invasion of 1650. The castle was finally taken when cannon damaged the upper part of the building.

Scalloway Castle *(opposite)*

Although an attractive-looking building, Scalloway's first owner was far from pleasant himself. A symbol of tyranny, the castle was built in 1600 by Patrick Stewart, Earl of Orkney and Lord of Shetland, to protect him as he exploited the inhabitants of the islands. The brutal oppressor was eventually indicted on seven charges of treason and he was executed in 1615.

INDEX